Music for Alto Saxophone & Piano

for

ADVANCED LEVEL
Volume 2

To access audio visit:
www.halleonard.com/mylibrary

Enter Code
7570-9431-7071-4564

ISBN 978-1-59615-594-7

Music Minus One

Exclusively Distributed By

HAL•LEONARD®

7777 W. BLUEMOUND RD. P.O. BOX 13819 MILWAUKEE, WI 53213

CONTENTS

PERFORMANCE GUIDE
COMMENTARY BY VINCENT ABATO

SCHUBERT
The Bee

This descriptive piece will be most effective if you master its technical difficulties before trying to play it up to tempo. The A sharp in the second measure will be easier if you use one and two. Use a chromatic fingering for the C. Observe the *poco a poco ritard,* and then work for a round, smooth tone for the measure marked *dolce.* When you have two slurred notes followed by a staccato, the second slurred note should be short. Exaggerate the staccato. You may wish to accent each triplet from measure 57 to the end.

RABAUD
Solo de Concours

You will need to look for natural resting or breathing places in the florid opening section. Do not make a big accelerando; it will be more satisfying from the musical standpoint if you keep it relaxed. The thirty-second notes in measure 11 should be played deliberately, not rushed.

If you do not ritard the end of the Largo section, the Allegro will be easier to establish. The Allegro needs a steady tempo. Resist the tendency to rush! The long trill on A sharp can be fingered with one and one or one and two, regular fingering.

Hold back the tempo a little when you get to the section in 6/8 time. The composer has written this piece in such a way that the change of meter (from 6/8 to 2/4) gives the effect of an accelerando. Keep the tempo constant, and play with a light touch. Use chromatic fingering for the chromatic scale. If you can't reach the high F sharp, do not be shy about playing it an octave lower.

CRESTON
Sonata for Alto Saxophone, Op. 19
2nd Movement: With tranquility

I was most fortunate in collaborating in the first performance of this work with the composer at the New York American Music Festival. Since then, we have played it together many times. Mr. Creston is a great modern composer, and through his friendship with the fine artist, Cecil Leeson, he has become prejudiced in favor of the saxophone.

If you follow the suggestions in the score, you will give a most effective performance of this Sonata. I would like to suggest one change: in the 14th measure, if you make the ritard on the second and third beats, and establish the tempo again on the fourth and fifth beats, measure 15 will have an easier flow. Notice the suggestion in measure 21: "increase a little." This crescendo should continue through the first three beats of measure 23; then, at the suggestion "softer," play a *subito piano*. Be aware that in this instance "increase" refers to volume, not tempo. When you come to the same suggestion in measure 24, it is coupled to an accelerando. There must be a gradual increase in volume all the way through the first note of measure 27. Exaggerate the thirty-second notes in measure 30. (The arpeggiated chord in the accompaniment will make it easy to stretch the dotted eighth note.) Notice how the saxophone in measure 31 is imitated by the piano in the next measure:

3rd Movement: With gaiety

If you exaggerate the accents and don't rush, you will capture the jazz/swing atmosphere the composer wants. (Remember, a more moderate tempo can be just as effective as a quick one!) Notice how the theme is repeated in various keys and with different rhythmic and harmonic backgrounds. You will need to listen carefully to the piano in measures 280 and 281. The saxophone continues the ascending scale, and you will need to match your dynamic level and work for a blend. You will want to give the last note an especially strong breath push!

The ending will be most effective if you try to play it without vibrato. Do not try to play so softly that you lose control!

THE BEE

FRANZ SCHUBERT
Trans. by Cecil Leeson

SOLO DE CONCOURS

HENRI RABAUD
Arr. and Edited by Harry Gee

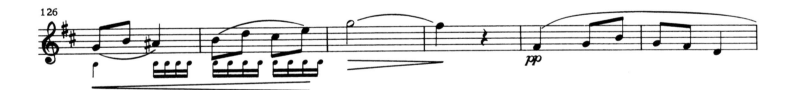

12

SONATA

II

♩ = 56 (4'18")

PAUL CRESTON
Op. 19

III

♩ = 126 (4'20")

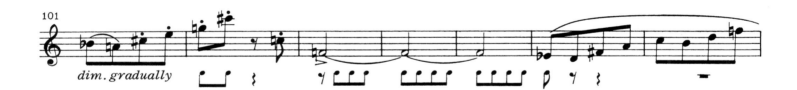

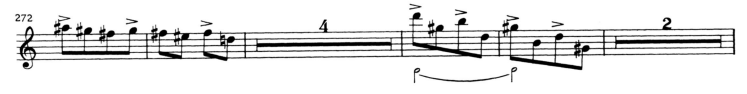

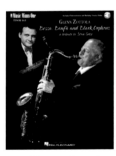
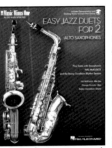